# Learning

# at

# Work

WITHDRAWN

**University**Campus
Oldham

A partnership between
the University of Huddersfield & Oldham College

WITHDRAWN

Library & Computing Centre: 0161 344 8888
UCO Main Reception: 0161 344 8800
Cromwell Street, Oldham,
OL1 1BB

This book is to be returned by the date on the self service receipt.
Your library account information can also be accessed online.

First Published in 1995

Kogan Page Limited
120 Pentonville Road
London N1 9JN

**British Library Cataloguing in Publication Data**

A CIP record for this book is available from the British Library.

ISBN 0 7494 1526 6

Typeset by The Bureau, Ruislip, Middlesex

Printed and bound in Great Britain by Biddles Ltd, Guildford and King's Lynn

# Contents

# Acknowledgements

This book owes a great deal to the vision, constructive criticism, guidance and experience of many people. Working with a wide mix of people, including managers, trainers, teachers, bus drivers, sewing machinists, prisoners, doctors, dentists, helicopter navigators and engineers, has resulted in comments and insights which put flesh onto the bones of the researches.

The original stimulus for the book came from senior managers in ICI including Peter Sinclair, who kindly wrote the section on Working with the group's ideas; Dai Williams and Ian Pearce. Mike Ing nursed the book through its presentation for ICI. Patricia Perry earns my grateful thanks for carrying out a great deal of the research with me at the University of Wales; Alan Downs for considerable argument and redrafting; Annabel Downs for managing me and Sue von Hirschfeld who has both contributed to the ideas and also used them extensively in South Africa.

Finally, my apologies and thanks to all those whom I should have named and have not. Without them, this book would have been the poorer.

# Introduction

The main purpose of this book is to air the problems encountered in learning, particularly as this affects the ability to change. Thus, although the intended audience is large and diverse, it tries to help the manager, the trainer and the learner (so that means all of us) to come to grips with the things which prevent learning and suggests some ways to remove or diminish these blockages.

A great deal of training in the past was concerned with rote learning repetitive tasks. People learned facts and procedures and practised the physical skills needed to carry out their jobs. The main learning skills used were those of memorisation, such as association, repetition and self-testing; and for physical skills, copying, part learning and practice.

The teaching or training of people has changed in line with the changing content of jobs. Work is now, to a far greater extent, carried out by small groups, each member of which is both dependent on the others and also has a degree of autonomy. The work is often concerned with monitoring what is going on, problem solving, planning, assessing priorities, influencing others and taking decisions.

Teaching and training now encompass the need to understand concepts and this has brought about fundamental changes in training and education. In its turn, the main learning skills involved have also radically changed to ones which link ideas to give understanding. While rote learning and skills training still have relevance, much training design is now concerned with organising material from which to develop concepts and a great deal of conceptual learning is helped by making mistakes and learning from them. Training enables people to do this in a safe and planned manner.

Experience, being the culmination of past learning, is a great help in learning something new, but can also be a major hindrance. It acts as a database with which to compare new learning, so we can distinguish if the new relates to and supplements our existing database, or is something outside it altogether. The hindrance comes when we are unwilling to see beyond our experience and either reject the new or distort it to fit our experience.

The ability to see that a concept is new and to adapt to it is obviously important. If, for example, a manufacturer of carbon paper viewed photocopying as a passing fad and continued blithely as before, then the company probably had a short future.

It is worth dwelling on this unfortunate maker of carbon paper for a while longer, because he or she illustrates on of those tiresome morals that some great aunts were fond of embroidering: "Change is only for the better if it improves us". Changes are brought to our notice as external happenings and often described vaguely so we do not always immediately grasp what they mean. External changes, however, more often than not, require internal changes and they can be dramatic ones. If, for example, you had learned, over a number of years, to become a master candle maker, the advent of electric (or even gas) light would probably leave you less than pleased. Almost overnight, the skills, social position and income you had spent years building up were redundant, diminished and gone. The more skilled and knowledgeable people are, the more reluctant they are likely to be to change what they do and, sadly, the quicker they will therefore fail. If, however, candle makers transformed themselves into makers of light fittings (often curiously reminiscent of candelabra) then they have recognised the effect of technical change and organised it to give them an entirely new venture with much more chance of success. Nowadays, the amount and rate of change and its increasing diversity and complexity can be daunting.

The need for continuous change in order to survive is widely recognised. Managers have an important role in both promoting and encouraging change, one essential of which is the development of people. This in turn depends largely on an encouragement and practice of active learning. But the job of manager, trainer or teacher is not to drive people to learn, but rather to promote the climate in which learner-driven learning can thrive. In these circumstances the learner can deal with change rather than meet it haplessly.

The intention of this book is to show how learner-driven learning can be encouraged and the material put into a context which promotes active learning.

The book has been written to be dipped into at any point, as most of the material, such as the beliefs and principles, is relevant to everyone. Sections 3, 4 and 7, however, have been particularly written for those designing training material; and Sections 5 and 6 have been written for both managers and trainers.

# The change equation

Among the reasons why change does not happen is the fact that no one has worked out the advantages and disadvantages, or the need relative to the pain involved in changing anything.

This has been described as the "change equation", which says that:-

If A + B + C is greater than D, then change is likely to happen.

If A + B + C is less than D, change is most unlikely.

Where   A =   Dissatisfaction with the present.

B =   Shared vision of the future.

C =   Knowledge of practical first steps.

D =   The costs of change in terms of effort, time, involvement and emotion.

This book is largely about item C in the change equation, that is, the practical first steps to help learning/change take place. We suggest you think of an area of dissatisfaction with the present and your vision of how you would like things to be in the future. Then, with help of this book review some practical first steps and what they might involve in terms of time, effort, involvement and emotion.

Here are two examples which occurred in different large organisations:-

## 1. Oil Company

**Dissatisfaction**        A tankover (spillage) every 47 days.

**Vision**        Few if any tankovers.

**Practical 1st Steps**
1. Two shift controllers, one operator, two craftsmen invited to a workshop.

2. Workshop as outlined (page 97) addressed the questions:-

   a) Why is it necessary to discuss tankover incidents?
   b) What do you believe causes them?
   c) What is the remedial measure for each identified cause?

**Cost**        2 hours of workshop time.

Manager carefully designing questions to be addressed.

Listening carefully and noting everything.

Following up ideas.

Acceptance of criticism - no blame.

**Outcome**
Core objective was achieved, namely to "blow away the clouds" that previously surrounded the subject of tankovers, to destroy the theory that they "just happened" and to identify and maximise awareness of the true fundamental causes. After 160 days there had been no tankover incident.

## 2. Pharmaceutical Company

**Dissatisfaction**     Production line throughput taking 6 weeks.

**Vision**     Production line throughput taking 2 weeks.

**Practical 1st Steps**     All persons involved on line attended workshop using pairs, systematic collection of ideas without comment. The question was addressed "What prevents production throughput taking less time?" After all possible causes were listed they were grouped and action plans produced.

**Cost**     Time to design workshop. Manager and operatives' time to attend workshop. Manager to listen and follow up suggestions. Be prepared to be open and honest and accept criticism.

**Outcome**
Production time reduced to 2 weeks.

Please use this page to list a dissatisfaction and vision you may have and with the help of this book think out the practical first steps and costs.

## Dissatisfaction

## Vision

## Practical 1st steps

## Costs

# Four beliefs about learning

**1.    Learning at work is largely a social activity.**

2.    Everyone has a role to play in helping people to learn.

3.    Everyone has something to contribute and something to gain when learning.

4.    Colleagues, trainers, parents and teachers sometimes unwittingly prevent people from learning.

Let us expand these four beliefs ...

14

## Belief 1

# Learning at work is largely a social activity

People leaving school for work find a very different view about learning. All through school time, there is a steady pressure to succeed as an individual learner. Tests and examinations assess how one person has fared against others. Positions in forms are given in school reports and categories of exam grades are proudly shown.

Some activities, such as team games, need co-operation between players, but this is a minor factor compared with the bulk of school learning.

At work, however, changes in technology have caused changes in the way work is organised. Teams are often formed in which everyone is dependent on every other team member. New entrants need to learn as quickly and thoroughly as possible for the sake of effectiveness and safety of the whole team. Learning in these circumstances is not competitive but social; as one person said "everybody **wanted** to help me be as good as they all were".

## Belief 1

# Learning at work is largely a social activity

## Myths

There is no difference in learning at school from learning at work.

It would be cheating to get someone else to help me.

Learning is a competitive activity.

In terms of learning, only about 10% of the population will succeed.

I do not like to ask questions because people will laugh at me.

16

## Belief 1

# Learning at work is largely a social activity

### Remedies

When introducing new people into a workplace, encourage them to talk to as many others as possible, such as the previous job-holder, their new boss and workmates.

Encourage people to try out ideas, express problems and compare with other situations they know about.

Encourage people to talk with others about what they have learned from media such as books, manuals, or computer-based material.

Demonstrate that learning is non-competitive by showing individual improvement and not comparisons between people.

Help everyone to achieve performance standards, rather than beat other people.

Demonstrate that sharing is not cheating and people learn more by sharing.

Make sure other people's viewpoints are sought as they are valuable in developing understanding.

# Four beliefs about learning

1. Learning at work is largely a social activity.

2. Everyone has a role to play in helping people to learn.

3. Everyone has something to contribute and something to gain when learning.

4. Colleagues, trainers, parents and teachers sometimes unwittingly prevent people from learning.

## Belief 2

# Everyone has a role to play in helping people to learn

It is not quite enough to realise that learning is a social activity if at the same time we think that only professional trainers and teachers can help us to learn.

As with a large number of things, who helps whom learn is not cut and dried. Sometimes, learning is best done in a classroom; sometimes, by distance learning; sometimes on-the-job with help from one's peers and management.

Sitting beside a skilled operative as a means of learning fell into disrepute probably because the emphasis was on "sit". In other words, the learner was expected to be passive and pick up the skill being taught by people who, in their day, learnt the same way and therefore were in danger of passing on bad practices.

Most work now needs far more active critical and co-operative learning, so those who are training others must expect questions, demands to see and understand and requests to go through it again.

Those training have, in their turn, to watch for the times when learners switch off; when they are puzzled, overwhelmed or just not understanding. At this point, everyone has a role in helping learners over the difficult bits. Different people will find different bits difficult.

## Belief 2

# Everyone has a role to play in helping people to learn

## Myths

Thinking that learning only takes place in a training department or college and only teachers and trainers can help people to learn.

Thinking it is not one's job to help new people to learn.

Thinking one has better things to do than sort out people's problems in doing the job - that is what the training department is for.

Securing one's position by deliberately not helping people to do their jobs better. ("I have to do everything around here".)

**Belief 2**

# Everyone has a role to play in helping people to learn

## Remedies

Encourage people to tell you what they already know.

Encourage people to tell you of similar things they have done.

Answer people's questions as simply and objectively as possible.

Check what is stopping/blocking their learning.

Check that people have understood by:

- getting them to explain it to you

- getting them to teach you

- asking a question such as "if ... happened what would be the effect?" the answer to which would have to be reasoned out.

Give as much positive feedback and encouragement as possible.

Arrange for people with different knowledge or skills to work in pairs in order to help each other.

Allow people to share their experiences of learning difficulties.

# Four beliefs about learning

1. Learning at work is largely a social activity.

2. Everyone has a role to play in helping people to learn.

3. Everyone has something to contribute and something to gain when learning.

4. Colleagues, trainers, parents and teachers sometimes unwittingly prevent people from learning.

**Belief 3**

# Everyone has something to contribute and something to gain when learning

Scenario: A group of people enter a classroom. They sit at individual desks facing a small rostrum behind which is a blackboard which has been inefficiently cleaned, so it looks like an abstract pattern in chalk.

A trainer enters the room and asks each person to state his or her name and then says his own. He then proceeds to lecture on safety factors related to factory equipment. Half the class looks bored to death; some of the rest look bewildered; one person takes notes and others pretend to while they in fact doodle.

This is a little overstated, but most of us would recognise that we have endured a lot of it at one time or another.

What is missing is any idea of the group of learners as individual people with their own ideas and contribution. The poor lecturer must be bored stiff, as he appears to give the same lecture over and over to a number of cardboard cutouts.

Seeing people as individuals lets everyone gain by finding out what they know and how they view things so the learning can begin at the right level and in terms understood by all. Then, for the lecturer to say as little as possible except when asked to explain. Who knows? We might end up with the group going out to look at the actual equipment, develop the safety factors and check their ideas with the supervisor. That might save a lot of doodles.

Finally, to make sure there are valid contributions to learning, the session has to be carefully structured to encourage people to contribute towards the precise learning topic.

**Belief 3**

# Everyone has something to contribute and something to gain when learning

## Myths

Assuming people have no relevant previous knowledge and experience.

Assuming that people are incapable of learning more.

Assuming that people are passive learners and ignoring the interactive process of learning.

Thinking that nothing will happen unless you begin it: e.g. people not learning until you take them in hand and teach them.

**Belief 3**

# Everyone has something to contribute and something to gain when learning

## Remedies

Ask people to:

- compare and contrast new ideas with their previous experience

- contribute through imagining what the effects of something might be

- think what the causes of something might be

- think of all the things that could go wrong

- look for similarities and differences between things

- think of the result if part of a procedure or system were omitted

- think of the effects of something not being done.

Listen to people's responses and relate what they say to the general topic.

Encourage further contributions by accepting and acknowledging each person's ideas.

Ask people for their ways of learning something such as names or dates and share these ways with other people.

# Four beliefs about learning

1. Learning at work is largely a social activity.

2. Everyone has a role to play in helping people to learn.

3. Everyone has something to contribute and something to gain when learning.

4. Colleagues, trainers, parents and teachers sometimes unwittingly prevent people from learning.

**Belief 4**

# Colleagues, trainers, parents and teachers sometimes unwittingly prevent people from learning

In a recent workshop, a group of managers came up with 71 statements of things which prevented people from learning. Thirty-three of these related to fears, worries and uncertainties within the person, which generally arose from past bad experiences of learning. Typical of these were "fear of looking foolish", "fear to say what I did not understand so I miss an essential step", "fear of any sort of assessment", and "fear of participation".

Twenty-seven of the responses were to do with the way the learning was designed or carried out. Among these were comments such as "the way the subject is taught", "the training is too complicated or too simple", "trainer not a good communicator, does not have the right knowledge and does not know how to train", "people punished for making mistakes", "impatience by trainer or other pupils", "too much training in one go" and "trainer is condescending".

All of this reinforces the fears, worries and uncertainties which may well have begun when a parent said "not now, dear, I am busy".

Helping people to learn is therefore not only dealing with the problems inherent in the learning, but also trying to avoid the behaviours which create or reinforce learning blocks.

27

## Belief 4

# Colleagues, trainers, parents and teachers sometimes unwittingly prevent people from learning

## Myths

Thinking you cannot teach old dogs new tricks.

Thinking lecturers are clever if they are difficult to understand.

Seeing the mistakes of others as a source of fun.

Assuming stress and worry always occur in learning.

Thinking everything has to be covered in the induction course.

Viewing questions as a disruption of learning or training.

Thinking everyone understands technical or in-house terms.

**Belief 4**

# Colleagues, trainers, parents and teachers sometimes unwittingly prevent people from learning

## Remedies

Make sure everyone has a clear idea of the objectives of the learning.

Get people to think about and say what prevents them learning and then think of ways to help them overcome their problems.

Check out what people already know and give them the information they need to fill any gaps.

Use the experiences of people to show how they can contribute.

Check that any technical words or phrases, jargon, or abbreviations that you use are understood.

Encourage openness and questioning by answering clearly and concisely.

Use mistakes/errors as learning oppotunities, such as asking for ideas about possible causes and remedies.

Be aware that some people experience learning blockages. They have difficulties in learning, not because they are stupid but because they may lack developed learning skills, be worried or feel insecure, not be good at concentrating, or have had bad experiences of learning.

Help the learners to accept that learning is not always easy and that often understanding does not take place for some time. A period of confusion is normal when new ideas are being learned, during which the learner must be helped to persevere.

# Questions on the four beliefs

You have now read about four beliefs. Would you think about them and decide:-

1. To what extent you agreed with them?

2. Did they remind you of events in your own experience? What were they?

3. What other beliefs, if any, would you add?

4. How might you use the "remedies", either for your own learning or helping others?

5. How could you check if you are actually using the "remedies"?

6. How might you assess the effectiveness of the ideas?

# Ten principles of learning

1. **Learners need to know where they are going and have a sense of progress towards their objectives.**

2. The learning environment has to be one of trust, respect, openness and acceptance of differences.

3. Being aware of and owning the responsibility for learning lies with the learner. Others can only give information, support and provide feedback.

4. Learners need to participate actively in the learning process.

5. Learning should be related to and use the learner's experience and knowledge.

6. Learning is not only a basic capability but also a group of skills which can be developed/learned.

7. Facts, concepts and skills are learned in different ways.

8. Getting ideas wrong can be a valuable aid to developing understanding.

9. For learning to be processed and assimilated, time must be allowed for reflection.

10. Effective learning depends on realistic, objective and constructive feedback.

## Principle 1

# Learners need to know where they are going and have a sense of progress towards their objectives

If people without any maps and little sense of direction set out to drive from Penzance to Whitehaven (or Moscow to Vladivostock, Cairo to Cape Town or New Orleans to Nova Scotia, for that matter ) it is unlikely they would arrive.

The major reasons for falling by the wayside are, first, no one has set up intermediate goals which indicate progress towards Whitehaven. Secondly, there are no signposts in Penzance directing travellers to Whitehaven.

The route has become easier over the years, (A30; M5; M6 to Penrith, junction 40; A66 to Bridgefoot; A595 to Whitehaven), but people still need to know how they are progressing towards their final goal.

Learners equally need to know their eventual aim; that is, where they are going. They have to map out how they are going to get there, what signs there will be along the way to show they are making progress and measures of how far they have got and how far they still have to go.

## Principle 1

# Learners need to know where they are going and have a sense of progress towards their objectives

## Pitfalls

"We thought it would do them good to have some training."

"I always compare a person's results with the best of other people's so that they will be motivated to try harder."

"We had a few spaces on the course, so we filled them with people who were not that busy."

"We never test during the course because it worries people so."

"I have been giving this course successfully for years so I know what is best for them."

"The beginning of a course is the wrong time to talk about the purposes or objectives of it."

## Principle 1

# Learners need to know where they are going and have a sense of progress towards their objectives

## Remedies

Base all training on a careful analysis of the learning needs. Where possible this should be stated in terms of desired knowledge or behaviour, for example "To use the computer for spreadsheets", rather than "To improve computer skills".

Clarify the purpose of the learning with the learner.

Check that the purpose lines up with the learner's own objectives.

Give benchmarks to show what is expected at various stages in learning.

Allow learners, where possible, to check their own progress against worked examples, models or check lists.

Remember to give **positive** feedback as well as negative.

When what is learned is related to speed, for example typing and sewing machining, then allow learners constantly to time themselves and chart their progress.

Where the final measure is to be a written test within a given time limit, give plenty of practice with mock papers under test conditions.

35

# Ten principles of learning

1. Learners need to know where they are going and have a sense of progress towards their objectives.

2. The learning environment has to be one of trust, respect, openness and acceptance of differences.

3. Being aware of and owning the responsibility for learning lies with the learner. Others can only give information, support and provide feedback.

4. Learners need to participate actively in the learning process.

5. Learning should be related to and use the learner's experience and knowledge.

6. Learning is not only a basic capability but also a group of skills which can be developed/learned.

7. Facts, concepts and skills are learned in different ways.

8. Getting ideas wrong can be a valuable aid to developing understanding.

9. For learning to be processed and assimilated, time must be allowed for reflection.

10. Effective learning depends on realistic, objective and constructive feedback.

**Principle 2**

# The learning environment has to be one of trust, respect, openness and acceptance of differences

This could well sound too Utopian to be part of the real world, so perhaps it might strike home a little more if we said "The learning environment has not to be one of distrust, lack of respect on either side, hidden manipulative behaviour and lack of tolerance for anything outside the norm".

From this, it is probably simpler to see that a learner would have to be determined indeed to be a success.

What the inverted statement indicates is that there should not be hidden agendas or assessments on anything but the apparent learning requirements. It should be known to everyone why they are there and what the learning will enable them to do.

Lack of respect on the trainer's side usually arises from the learners' side, by being talked down to, not listened to and being treated generally as second class citizens.

All of the positive factors mentioned help dismantle the blocks most learners have towards learning and all the negative factors help reinforce and build higher the resistance many people have to being taught.

## Principle 2

# The learning environment has to be one of trust, respect, openness and acceptance of differences

**Pitfalls**

Holding the view that:

"There is one best way of instructing, learning or doing something."

"I think people need to be strictly disciplined while they are learning."

"These young people have had a difficult time of it so I praise everything they do to build up their confidence."

"When I think someone is day-dreaming I ask them a question to catch them out."

"I was horrified to find people talking during their project work - they cannot have been learning."

"I have found that people ask questions just to appear clever or disrupt the lesson."

38

**Principle 2**

# The learning environment has to be one of trust, respect, openness and acceptance of differences

## Remedies

Give objective and realistic feedback.

Listen to people's ideas before telling them your views.

Where possible accept things can be done in a number of ways.

Encourage people to value the contributions of others irrespective of status.

Encourage people to identify their errors and how to overcome them, then praise them for realistic appraisal.

Listen to and answer questions carefully.

When in a group try to avoid either praising or criticising any individual; make these points one-to-one.

Encourage all to contribute by collecting ideas systematically before any discussion takes place.

If the group members are reluctant to participate, set up pair working, so that ideas come from the pair and are not identified with an individual.

If the group is reluctant to ask questions, suggest that these are put on slips of paper so that the questions are anonymous.

# Ten principles of learning

1.  Learners need to know where they are going and have a sense of progress towards their objectives.

2.  The learning environment has to be one of trust, respect, openness and acceptance of differences.

3.  **Being aware of and owning the responsibility for learning lies with the learner. Others can only give information, support and provide feedback.**

4.  Learners need to participate actively in the learning process.

5.  Learning should be related to and use the learner's experience and knowledge.

6.  Learning is not only a basic capability but also a group of skills which can be developed/learned.

7.  Facts, concepts and skills are learned in different ways.

8.  Getting ideas wrong can be a valuable aid to developing understanding.

9.  For learning to be processed and assimilated, time must be allowed for reflection.

10. Effective learning depends on realistic, objective and constructive feedback.

## Principle 3

# Being aware of and owning the responsibility for learning lies with the learner. Others can only give information, support and provide feedback

Some time ago, research showed that poor learners tended to be passive towards learning and saw learning as someone else's responsibility. They were also unsure about the different ways of learning, so anyone else taking responsibility let them do nothing rather than get in a hopeless mess. If they were passive at school, with luck (and luck, here, was often with them) the teachers would take on the responsibility for learning. The teachers would tell them what to learn, how to learn it and check to see that it was learned.

If the learners wanted to please their teachers or felt "anything for a quiet life" they might do what they were told. The purpose of doing so was, perhaps, "a quiet life" and not to add to their body of knowledge or to help them solve a problem.

Learning can be an arduous, if not painful process and learners must want to learn. To do so, they have to accept responsibility for organising themselves and other resources in order to learn. Others can help but learners have actively to seek out and organise the help.

41

**Principle 3**

# Being aware of and owning the responsibility for learning lies with the learner. Others can only give information, support and provide feedback

This is all the instructor's fault. He should have explained it better.

**Pitfalls**

"If I have not learned it is the trainer's fault."

"If I have not understood something, I must cover it up and not admit it."

"Not knowing, or asking questions, means I am stupid."

"I should not demand better training."

"I should not point out that the methods of instruction are not helping me to learn."

"I should not demand better manuals or training aids."

"I am thick and not much good at learning."

**Principle 3**

# Being aware of and owning the responsibility for learning lies with the learner. Others can only give information, support and provide feedback

## Remedies

Believe that everyone has the capacity to learn.

Help people to identify ways of learning which are appropriate for what is being learned, e.g. facts that need to be memorised.

Develop and get people to practise a range of ways of learning, e.g. self-testing, grouping, linking and questioning.

Allow people to query how they are being taught.

Encourage people to accept responsibility by getting them to plan and assess their own learning.

Give feedback which relates to specific actions or points, so people know how to correct themselves or why they are doing well.

Give feedback which can be understood. Check that people know any technical terms you are using.

Give feedback which is honest and can be seen to be so.

Only criticise if a positive proposal for improvement can be made.

# Ten principles of learning

1.  Learners need to know where they are going and have a sense of progress towards their objectives.

2.  The learning environment has to be one of trust, respect, openness and acceptance of differences.

3.  Being aware of and owning the responsibility for learning lies with the learner. Others can only give information, support and provide feedback.

4.  Learners need to participate actively in the learning process.

5.  Learning should be related to and use the learner's experience and knowledge.

6.  Learning is not only a basic capability but also a group of skills which can be developed/learned.

7.  Facts, concepts and skills are learned in different ways.

8.  Getting ideas wrong can be a valuable aid to developing understanding.

9.  For learning to be processed and assimilated, time must be allowed for reflection.

10. Effective learning depends on realistic, objective and constructive feedback.

**Principle 4**

# Learners need to participate actively in the learning process

The need for learners to be responsible for their learning has been described. Moving forward into the learning process itself, there has to be a careful balance between learners and resources. If this balance is not achieved, there is a danger that the learners could slip back into passive dependency.

The major role of, say, a trainer, is therefore to organise the learning experience beforehand in such a way that the learners can learn and actively participate in the experience. The trainer, during the learning process, then becomes a resource to provide opportunities, clarify objectives, answer questions, collect ideas from the learners and give feedback.

A major difference is that, as a resource, the trainer is unobtrusive until asked to help or respond in some way. The trainer's main skill is therefore in preparing and not in performing.

**Principle 4**

# Learners need to participate actively in the learning process

## Pitfalls

"I allow them to ask questions at the end".

"They use the keyboard to answer multiple choice questions".

"When giving a talk I use the 'pounce' method to keep them on their toes".

"I tell them to go away and study the manual".

"I get them to find things out through experience".

**Principle 4**

# Learners need to participate actively in the learning process

## Remedies

Set problems within the learners' capability and where the solution provides new insight and understanding.

Encourage questions before giving information. This enables the information to be linked into the learner's needs and ideas.

Encourage planning and listing priorities.

Let people, where possible in pairs, learn by thinking of purposes, making comparisons, identifying causes and effects, anticipating problems and imagining "what if?"

Help learners to identify their needs and how they will assess that these have been achieved.

Design self-assessment quizzes with model answers provided.

Ask people to suggest how they could help others.

Encourage people to describe ways that their learning could be helped.

Get groups to design quizzes for other groups; for example, trainee salesmen learning about products.

Encourage reflection after a learning experience such as a lecture or presentation. This can be done by asking people what they have learned, to precis what they have heard or to describe some applications or implications.

# Ten principles of learning

1.  Learners need to know where they are going and have a sense of progress towards their objectives.

2.  The learning environment has to be one of trust, respect, openness and acceptance of differences.

3.  Being aware of and owning the responsibility for learning lies with the learner. Others can only give information, support and provide feedback.

4.  Learners need to participate actively in the learning process.

5.  Learning should be related to and use the learner's experience and knowledge.

6.  Learning is not only a basic capability but also a group of skills which can be developed/learned.

7.  Facts, concepts and skills are learned in different ways.

8.  Getting ideas wrong can be a valuable aid to developing understanding.

9.  For learning to be processed and assimilated, time must be allowed for reflection.

10. Effective learning depends on realistic, objective and constructive feedback.

## Principle 5

# Learning should be related to and use the learner's experience and knowledge

A great deal of our learning amounts to an increase in our databank. It may be, for example, that having a body of knowledge and experience in woodworking tools and simple joints, we can extend this to making a mortise and tenon joint. If, however, we had no such experience and thought chisels were screwdrivers, then our attempts at the mortise and tenon could be disastrous. More realistically, we would not begin to try.

The woodworking illustration is an obvious step from simple to more complex operations. Sometimes the connection is less obvious, where, for example, we are used to thinking in a certain way which enables us to tackle new concepts.

In garden fetes there is often a tank of water with an object at the bottom. People try to grasp the object and find that they are some distance off. They can fish around until they strike the object by chance or stop to think why their perception was wrong. In the former, they will learn little. In the latter case, they will begin to form concepts about the refraction of light. Without, however, the initial experience of the object in water, some of us would find the abstract idea of refraction very difficult to grasp.

When helping people to learn we have to balance the need for theory to follow experience and facts to precede understanding.

**Principle 5**

# Learning should be related to and use the learner's experience and knowledge

## Pitfalls

"I assume they all know nothing and spend a lot of time on first principles."

"I do not find out about my trainees in advance as I like to treat them all the same."

"The group is too large to meet the needs of individuals."

"I have been giving this lecture successfully in the college for several years."

**Principle 5**

# Learning should be related to and use the learner's experience and knowledge

## Remedies

Always check out the learner's previous experience and knowledge.

Draw on the learner's experience to link with the new ideas.

Use experienced group members to help others to learn.

Encourage people to give accounts from their own experience to help others to understand.

Get learners to compare and contrast old and new experiences.

Help people to form concepts from their own and others' experiences (for example on safety, quality, tolerances) and relate these to generally accepted principles.

Use anecdotes and stories relevant to people's experience to explain concepts and then relate these concepts to the new situations. Fables and parables, for example, convey underlying principles. In the same way, examples of accidents help to develop an understanding of safety principles.

# Ten principles of learning

1.  Learners need to know where they are going and have a sense of progress towards their objectives.

2.  The learning environment has to be one of trust, respect, openness and acceptance of differences.

3.  Being aware of and owning the responsibility for learning lies with the learner. Others can only give information, support and provide feedback.

4.  Learners need to participate actively in the learning process.

5.  Learning should be related to and use the learner's experience and knowledge.

6.  Learning is not only a basic capability but also a group of skills which can be developed/learned.

7.  Facts, concepts and skills are learned in different ways.

8.  Getting ideas wrong can be a valuable aid to developing understanding.

9.  For learning to be processed and assimilated, time must be allowed for reflection.

10. Effective learning depends on realistic, objective and constructive feedback.

## Principle 6

# Learning is not only a basic capability but also a group of skills which can be developed/learned

From common experience, most would agree that the capability to learn differs from person to person, both in its extent and by subject. Some, for example, have an aptitude for languages and others for art.

Irrespective of our starting points, all of us can use the same skills to improve our learning. Indeed, the definition of skill emphasises that it is something that, with practice, improves.

A problem immediately arises in identifying the skills of learning because they are internalised processes used in improving knowledge or understanding. The knowledge or understanding gained are the products of using the processes of learning and are not, therefore, themselves skills.

A second problem arises because of a confusion between learning styles and the skills of learning. There is ample evidence that people have preferred styles of learning and can learn more easily if material is presented to them in a manner suited to their style preference. At the same time, irrespective of preferred style, all learners use, or have available to them, the same skills of learning.

Last, (and this will be amplified in the next principle), the skills of learning are different, dependent on the needs of the subject matter.

By application of the relevant learning skills to the subject to be learned, one can move up a hierarchy of knowledge. Each stage builds on the previous one, using the process skills of learning.

53

## Principle 6

# Learning is not only a basic capability but also a group of skills which can be developed/learned

## Pitfalls

"I am no good at learning."

"They are thick."

"I always help David because he finds it so difficult."

"Just concentrate on what you have got to learn."

"Our job is to get them NVQs."

## Principle 6

# Learning is not only a basic capability but also a group of skills which can be developed/learned

### Remedies

Training should be given so that the best ways of learning can be used by the learner e.g. plenty of practice and feedback for physical skills, self-testing cards for memorising facts, problem solving to help understanding. (See Section 3 on designing training material.)

Trainers must present information related to appropriate ways of learning.

Trainers should help people to develop their learning skills e.g. memorising and questioning.

Trainers should set tasks which stretch people.

Trainers must have positive expectations of people and never belittle or break them.

People should spend time thinking of the "how" of learning as well as the "what".

For learning skills to be used appropriately and deliberately they have to be made overt.

Trainers must include periods for learners to think about what they have learned, how they have learned it and how they can apply it.

Encourage learners when reading or listening to a lecture to ask themselves questions such as: "What is the purpose?" "What in my experience does this relate to?" "What would be the effect of the opposite?" "How could I apply the idea?" "How could I test out the ideas?"

55

# Ten principles of learning

1.  Learners need to know where they are going and have a sense of progress towards their objectives.

2.  The learning environment has to be one of trust, respect, openness and acceptance of differences.

3.  Being aware of and owning the responsibility for learning lies with the learner. Others can only give information, support and provide feedback.

4.  Learners need to participate actively in the learning process.

5.  Learning should be related to and use the learner's experience and knowledge.

6.  Learning is not only a basic capability but also a group of skills which can be developed/learned.

7.  **Facts, concepts and skills are learned in different ways.**

8.  Getting ideas wrong can be a valuable aid to developing understanding.

9.  For learning to be processed and assimilated, time must be allowed for reflection.

10. Effective learning depends on realistic, objective and constructive feedback.

**Principle 7**

# Facts, concepts and skills are learned in different ways

This seems a relatively simple idea, because no one would try to understand a telephone number, or try to memorise why night falls. On reflection, however, some might memorise statements about why night falls instead of trying to understand the reason.

While, therefore, we cannot memorise facts by trying to understand them, there is the problem that we can sometimes memorise statements about concepts instead of understanding them. Although we can regurgitate what we have memorised, we are not in a position to use the concept to develop further concepts. If we were faced with the question "why are nights in the UK sometimes shorter and sometimes longer?" we could not necessarily answer this from our memorised statements about night falling.

There are several methods we can use to memorise facts, but we must be careful to distinguish between facts and concepts, which need completely different ways of learning.

When learning physical skills such as riding a bike we must experience and practise the skill. Memorising the parts of a bicycle or understanding momentum and gravity will not give us the skill of cycling.

To help people distinguish between different ways of learning, a mnemonic was formed as follows:

Facts need **M**emorising

Concepts need **U**nderstanding

Physical Skills need **D**oing

Hence "**MUD**".

## Principle 7

# Facts, concepts and skills are learned in different ways

## Pitfalls

"Don't worry about what it means, first learn it."

"You can memorise everything."

"You should understand everything."

## Principle 7

# Facts, concepts and skills are learned in different ways

### Remedies

Be aware that facts are concrete things one can be told and they can be memorised.

Be aware that everybody needs to formulate concepts for themselves.

Memorise by experimenting with different methods, such as repeating, self-testing, visualising, grouping and associating.

Avoid getting facts such as telephone numbers, dates and formulae wrong by learning them in parts and checking accuracy immediately.

Develop concepts by:-

- Clarifying the purpose of what one wishes to understand;
- Experiencing things;
- Reflecting on experiences;
- Comparing and contrasting things;
- Looking at things from other people's viewpoints;
- Imagining "what if ...?";
- Imagining problems, causes and effects;
- Checking out ideas under new or different circumstances.

These approaches we call "keys to understanding" (see page 85).

# Ten principles of learning

1.  Learners need to know where they are going and have a sense of progress towards their objectives.

2.  The learning environment has to be one of trust, respect, openness and acceptance of differences.

3.  Being aware of and owning the responsibility for learning lies with the learner. Others can only give information, support and provide feedback.

4.  Learners need to participate actively in the learning process.

5.  Learning should be related to and use the learner's experience and knowledge.

6.  Learning is not only a basic capability but also a group of skills which can be developed/learned.

7.  Facts, concepts and skills are learned in different ways.

8.  **Getting ideas wrong can be a valuable aid to developing understanding.**

9.  For learning to be processed and assimilated, time must be allowed for reflection.

10. Effective learning depends on realistic, objective and constructive feedback.

**Principle 8**

# Getting ideas wrong can be a valuable aid to developing understanding

First, we must distinguish clearly between getting a fact wrong and getting ideas wrong. We probably have all suffered at some time or other from knowing we make an error of fact, but not knowing which of two versions is the wrong one. Then, most likely, we choose the wrong one yet again. We first think, for example, that someone is named John and then find his name is Jim. We tend to remember both names, but are uncertain which is right and which is wrong. The difficulty of unlearning and relearning makes it very important to do our utmost to learn facts correctly from the word go.

When we come to ideas, however, we have a very different position. We need to extend beyond the tramlines of accepted ideas in order to expand our concepts. Experience is a valuable starting point, provided we do not allow it to limit us. There is an old cliche about experience which says "he spent the first year learning all the wrong ways and the next twenty practising them."

What we have to do is evaluate our experience against new concepts to see if it is both relevant and fitting. The danger comes when we try to force concepts to fit our previous experience rather than adapt our experience to new data and concepts. The mix of dogmatic experience and associated concepts can be a potent brew to overcome, as Darwin found.

So we need to push our ideas until we fall into error and be aware when we are wrong in order to reassess and reform our concepts. It is at that point of realisation of error that we often make considerable advances in our concepts. Unlike the uncertainties we might face over the correctness of facts, once we have altered or expanded our concepts, we are never confused by our past concepts. We may, for example, think all swans are white until we meet a black one. From that moment our concept about swans changes.

61

## Principle 8

# Getting ideas wrong can be a valuable aid to developing understanding

## Pitfalls

"I try to avoid something I have not done before."

"I never do anything unless I have had prior approval."

"I consider learning is about not making mistakes."

"It seems rude to ask questions."

"When I make a mistake I quickly cover it up and try to forget about it."

## Principle 8

# Getting ideas wrong can be a valuable aid to developing understanding

## Remedies

Encourage people to be adventurous in their ideas so that, when the ideas are tested, any errors they discover will expand their understanding. Where safety is concerned get people to check their ideas with an experienced person **before** testing them in practice.

Get people to recognise where an error in understanding has occurred; what the error is; and re-think the position. In so doing, understanding is increased.

Encourage the sharing of learning from mistakes.

Use the mistakes of others to help people think through the probable causes, what could have prevented them and what to do if similar mistakes occur.

Use mistakes and their causes to develop concepts, rules and procedures.

For these remedies in particular to work, there must be a learning environment of trust, respect, openness and acceptance of differences (Principle 2).

# Ten principles of learning

1. Learners need to know where they are going and have a sense of progress towards their objectives.

2. The learning environment has to be one of trust, respect, openness and acceptance of differences.

3. Being aware of and owning the responsibility for learning lies with the learner. Others can only give information, support and provide feedback.

4. Learners need to participate actively in the learning process.

5. Learning should be related to and use the learner's experience and knowledge.

6. Learning is not only a basic capability but also a group of skills which can be developed/learned.

7. Facts, concepts and skills are learned in different ways.

8. Getting ideas wrong can be a valuable aid to developing understanding.

9. For learning to be processed and assimilated, time must be allowed for reflection.

10. Effective learning depends on realistic, objective and constructive feedback.

## Principle 9

# For learning to be processed and assimilated, time must be allowed for reflection

Something most of us remember from schooldays is a breathless scamper from one classroom to another, from Latin to Mathematics, or, if we stayed in one classroom, a breathless scamper by one teacher and another. What there seemed little opportunity for was any form of review or reflection on what had just transpired. Perhaps that explains a stubborn belief that quadratic equations have something to do with mustering troops for the Gallic Wars.

There may well be all sorts of other confusions in people's minds when new information and concepts follow each other in rapid succession without the vital pauses for reflection. If we are allowed these pauses, we can integrate the new with past knowledge and concepts and see how it fits in and increases our bank of knowledge.

## Principle 9

# For learning to be processed and assimilated, time must be allowed for reflection

## Pitfalls

"We've got a lot to get through, so there won't be time for questions."

"You all understood that, didn't you?"

"That is my twentieth and concluding point and I am sorry I now have to rush away."

"We must move on quickly to the next subject."

## Principle 9

# For learning to be processed and assimilated, time must be allowed for reflection

## Remedies

Keep in mind the Kolb learning cycle:

**EXPERIENCE** is followed by reflection and observation

**REFLECTION** and observation leads to

**FORMULATION** of abstract concepts and generalisations, the implications of which are tested in new situations through

**ACTIVE EXPERIMENTATION** which brings us back to experience

Allow ponder periods for people to reflect on what they have learned and how it can be applied.

Encourage people to share and discuss their ideas. When these are being systematically collected, people can reflect on each one and learn from them.

After ponder periods, check out what people have learned, by encouraging everyone, including the tutor, to give feedback.

# Ten principles of learning

1.  Learners need to know where they are going and have a sense of progress towards their objectives.

2.  The learning environment has to be one of trust, respect, openness and acceptance of differences.

3.  Being aware of and owning the responsibility for learning lies with the learner. Others can only give information, support and provide feedback.

4.  Learners need to participate actively in the learning process.

5.  Learning should be related to and use the learner's experience and knowledge.

6.  Learning is not only a basic capability but also a group of skills which can be developed/learned.

7.  Facts, concepts and skills are learned in different ways.

8.  Getting ideas wrong can be a valuable aid to developing understanding.

9.  For learning to be processed and assimilated, time must be allowed for reflection.

10. **Effective learning depends on realistic, objective and constructive feedback.**

## Principle 10

# Effective learning depends on realistic, objective and constructive feedback

This is one of those principles which is easy to agree with and the very devil to unravel. So let us take it one adjective at a time.

Realistic feedback must mean that it should relate to factual, concrete, observable things. In trainability tests, for example, lists are developed of errors in procedures, sequences, use of tools and of any end product. All these are observable aspects which affect the total job.

Objective feedback implies two things. First, that feedback is not biased by personal feelings or anything else which is not essential to a judgement. Second, that there are criteria against which feedback is given.

The third adjective is 'constructive' which means that any critical feedback should indicate what steps should be taken to improve, or why something is good so that it can be repeated.

In woodworking terms, for example, a loose half-lap 'T' joint could be shown by the degree and effect of its looseness (realistic and objective feedback) and that the problem arose from not sawing on the waste side of the line (constructive feedback). Ideally, of course, it would be of benefit to the learner if he or she could identify all these points.

69

**Principle 10**

# Effective learning depends on realistic, objective and constructive feedback

## Pitfalls

"I always praise people because I would only demotivate them by telling them the truth about their performance."

"Praise gives people swollen heads."

"I mark their work 'Excellent, good, fair, not good enough, failed'."

"You only have to achieve a pass rate."

**Principle 10**

# Effective learning depends on realistic, objective and constructive feedback

## Remedies

Give feedback which relates to specific actions or points, so people know how to correct themselves or why they are doing well.

Give feedback which can be understood.

Check that people know any technical terms you are using.

Give feedback which is honest and can be seen to be so.

Only criticise if a proposal for improvement can be suggested.

Make sure people have the time and any facilities needed to make use of the feedback.

Give examples of model answers or work pieces.

Where scoring is in marks, list the variables being assessed and the portion of marks given to each variable, for example, presentation, content, logic, grammar and spelling.

Ask learners to design methods of assessment and then assess and discuss each other's work.

# Questions on the ten principles

You have now read about the ten principles. Would you think about them and decide:-

1. To what extent you agreed with them?

2. Did they remind you of events in your own experiences?

3. What other principles, if any, would you add?

4. How might you use the "remedies", either for your own learning or helping others?

5. How could you check if you are actually using "remedies"?

6. How might you assess the effectiveness of the ideas?

# Designing training material for learning

Principle 7 distinguishes between facts we need to memorise, concepts we need to understand and physical skills we learn by doing.

Life, however, is seldom if ever clearcut and many things we have to learn include all three aspects of MUD (page 57). In driving a car, for example, we memorise road signs so that we can be aware that we have to give way to traffic to our right on a roundabout just ahead. We make constant judgements based on our appreciation (or understanding) of what other drivers are doing or are likely to do: what adult and child pedestrians and animals are around and their possible behaviour. Finally, we have the physical skills involved in handling the car and its controls.

Learning all this needs a careful meshing of physical skills, understanding and memorising. To achieve this, the training material has to be carefully thought out and designed to give learners the information, experiences and practice they need while presenting this diversity in the different ways that best help the learner to learn.

Because we use different mental processes for learning different types of things it is important to design material which matches process to product.

This section covers **designing training material for:**

> **Physical skills**
>
> **Sensory discriminations and assessment**
>
> **Facts**
>
> **Procedures**

73

# Physical skills

Learning physical skills involves a good model, breaking the skill down, practice to mastery and feedback.

## Pitfalls

"I let them learn by trial and error."

"When they can do a straight weld a few times we immediately move them on."

"I get them to watch how the others do it and then they go away and try it out."

# Physical skills

## Remedies

Let them watch a video, which can be slowed down in order to clarify what the skill is and how to break it down.

Break the task into parts.

Arrange for learners to practise each part to a high standard of speed and accuracy.

Expect learning plateaus to occur. This is often the stage when people are unconsciously learning to use information from muscles as well as from their eyes and ears. Using this muscle information is much quicker than using other cues. Once this is established they will start to improve and often find they can do things without thinking.

When practising, ensure they can get feedback on what they are doing. This could be from mirrors, video tape, tape recordings or other people.

Make sure they practise until they get it right every time.

Do not let them learn bad ways. Unlearning of physical skills is difficult and time consuming.

# Sensory discriminations and assessment

Learning to discriminate not only involves sensory skills but also understanding the implications of what we see, hear, taste, touch or smell.

## Pitfalls

"You only pick these things up with experience."

"If I show people the most likely faults they will pick them up."

"I tell them to listen to their engine."

# Sensory discriminations and assessment

## Remedies

When learning to discriminate, begin by comparing gross differences; for example, the sound of a labouring engine when a gear change is overdue compared with a correct engine sound. Then finer discriminations can be introduced and practised.

Draw the learner's attention to the clues that experienced people use; for example the sound of a faulty bearing, the colour of a patient's skin, the smell from an oven, the taste of a wine or the feel of a vibration.

Let learners check out with an experienced person their assessment of something before being told the expert's assessment.

Let learners assess a number of faults by comparing faulty items with a model - noticing differences and developing ideas about likely faults.

Give the learners a number of faulty items and get them to work out causes and effects.

Check their knowledge of standards and their understanding of the reasons for the standards and why they might vary.

# Facts

Learning facts is rather like learning a physical skill, as it involves breaking the task down, practice to mastery and feedback. It is considerably helped by consciously using certain strategies.

## Pitfalls

"Memorising things is not important."

"I do not see that teaching ways of memorising is part of my job."

"I give them the manual and tell them to learn for themselves."

# Facts

## Remedies

Clearly identify facts that must be memorised.

Prevent errors in the early stages, possibly by breaking up the material and learning it in parts.

Be aware of visual, aural and tactile imagery according to individual preferences e.g. do you "see", "hear" or "feel" your telephone number?

Encourage learners to make up associations or mnemonics or group things.

Use self-testing cards to encourage constant testing and self-testing.

Get people to design their own memory joggers such as flow diagrams, lists and performance aids.

Reinforce material learned by saying or writing. Use media for reinforcement by listening, viewing or reading.

Help older learners by encouraging them to revise the things they have already memorised while learning the new material.

Use number rhyme systems for learning lists. First memorise associations between numbers and rhyming objects (e.g. one - bun, two - shoe, three - tree, and so on). Then form unusual visual associations between the things to be remembered and the rhyming objects.

Have a strong mental picture of a large house with a number of different rooms, passages and stairways which you can "walk through" in your mind. Then associate each window, doorway or cupboard with an idea or thing which you want to remember.

# Procedures

Learning a procedure not only includes what it is, but understanding the implications of not following the procedure and how to check it has been carried out correctly.

## Pitfalls

"They do not need to know why they do it."

"They can just pick it up from experience."

"We cut out the warning buzzer because it was often going off when there was nothing wrong."

# Procedures

## Remedies

Get the learners to work out the actual sequence for themselves by observation of someone carrying it out.

Ask "What can go wrong?" if any stage is omitted.

The trainer carries out the sequence with minor errors which learners have to identify. They then have to work out the consequences.

Learners think of ways in which they can ensure they have carried out each step correctly and make up their own checklists or performance aids.

Learners check their learning by teaching an experienced person.

Silently demonstrate the procedure, encouraging the learners to ask whatever questions they like. Tell them they will be expected to describe or follow the procedure afterwards.

# Designing training material to develop understanding

Because we use different mental processes for learning different types of things it is important to design material which matches process to product.

Concepts, unlike facts, cannot easily be told directly. We have to use various ways of helping people to form concepts for themselves.

**Concepts can be developed by using training material based on:**

**Deduction**

**Questions based on the keys to understanding**

**Using solutions to problems**

**Using the causes of problems**

**Using comparisons**

**Gaining insight through experience**

# Learning concepts

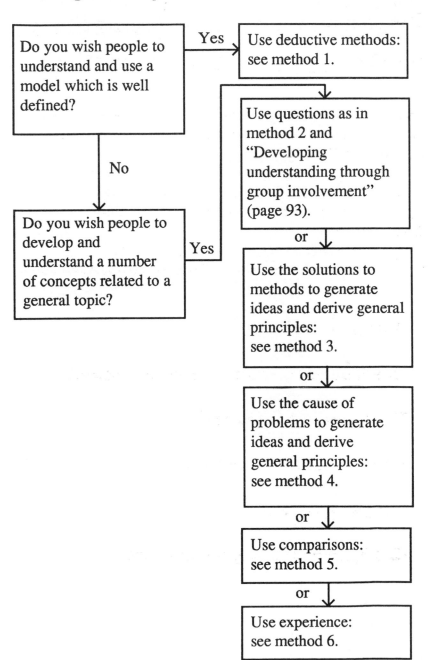

## Method 1

# Deduction

This is only appropriate if there is a defined model or concept to be understood.

1. Give people the shape of the model and tell them they will have to work out the generic labels of its parts.

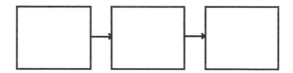

2. Then give three completed models and tell people to compare and contrast the same parts of two models and work out what the labels could stand for. Then check their ideas out with the third. Carrying on this way they work out the concepts for themselves and complete their blank model.

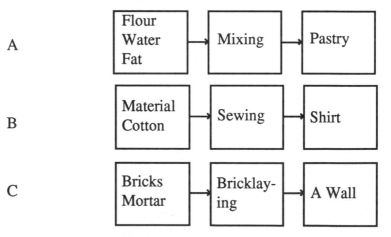

A   Flour / Water / Fat → Mixing → Pastry

B   Material / Cotton → Sewing → Shirt

C   Bricks / Mortar → Bricklaying → A Wall

3. They are given a completed model to check against their own.

Input → Activity → Product

## Method 2

# Questions based on the keys to understanding

Developing a greater degree of understanding can be helped by using certain questions which we call **"keys"** designed to increase our database by generating a large body of ideas.

We have called the approaches **"keys"** because each gives entry to some understanding, although all of them may not be relevant for every occasion. Most involve ways of questioning either the person's own knowledge or experience, or that of other people.

If you wish to ask questions based on the keys it is helpful to ask them in a particular order so that ideas are first broadly expanded before narrowing down to specific details.

First, one may need to clarify what one wishes to understand by questions about the **purpose or definition**.

Then one can broaden ideas by using questions involving **comparisons and viewpoints**.

Questions about **problems** or **"what if?"** help to develop understanding of issues which need to be tackled; however, they can limit ideas if introduced too early.

Having identified problems, ways of overcoming them need to be found and this leads to specific action planning.

As part of this process it is helpful to design **checking questions**.

## Method 2
# Questions based on the keys to understanding

### Basic forms of questions based on the keys

**Purpose**         -    What are the reasons for ... ?
                    -    What are the purposes of ... ?
                    -    Why do ... ?

**Viewpoints**      -    How is ... seen by ... ?
                    -    How is ... viewed by ... ?
                    -    How does ... looked to ... ?

**Comparisons**     -    How will "x" be similar to, or different from "y"?
                    -    How does "x" need to differ from "y"?
                    -    How does "x" differ from other forms of "x" (e.g. measurement, interviews, tests)?

**Problems**        -    What could prevent ... ?
                    -    What are all the things that could go wrong?
                    -    What could stop ... ?

**What if?**        -    What if ... were left out?
                    -    What if ... fail to arrive?
                    -    What if a competitor ... ?

**Checks**          -    How can we measure if ... ?
                    -    How can we show if we have ... ?
                    -    What would be the implications of ... ?

## Method 3
# Using solutions to problems

Present a number of scenarios all of which are faulty in some way and ask people to work out why they are faulty. From this, derive general principles.

For example, to learn the things to take into account when designing experiments in psychology, five scenarios were presented. The learners were told that all the experiments had flaws in their design. They were asked, working in pairs, to work out what the experimental flaws were and then to check with the tutor's list. Finally, they derived the necessary principles for designing experiments.

An example of one of the scenarios is:

**"Learning a Poem"**

> *An experiment was carried out to find out which of two methods was the better way of learning a poem. Students were divided into two groups: Group A comprised 10 people (5 males and 5 females) from the English Department and Group B comprised 12 people (7 males and 5 females) from the Engineering Department. Groups were matched according to age and academic qualifications.*

> *In order that each group would be motivated to learn a poem, they were given a chance of selecting one themselves. They were to learn 8 lines (lines comparable in length). Group A chose from "Spike Milligan's Poems" while Group B selected from "Shakespeare".*

## Method 3
# Using solutions to problems

*Group A was instructed to learn the poem in any way they wished while Group B were asked to learn the poem two lines at a time, and only when they had learned the two lines to go on to the next two. They were all given 15 minutes to learn the poem. After 15 minutes they were asked to write the poem down from memory: the results were collected.*

*Results showed that Group A did significantly better than Group B. The researchers concluded that leaving the students to decide their own styles of learning was more effective than giving them a style. What do you think?*

## Method 4

# Using the causes of problems

A tutor selects a topic which is relevant to the group; for example, it could be safety, social skills, machine faults and so on; and describes accidents or incidents within the topic which could have been caused by many factors.

The tutor asks participants, working in pairs, to take each incident or accident in turn and think of every possible reason for the incident or accident.

Share all the ideas.

Ask the group in pairs to generate some principles to prevent or remedy the described accidents or incidents. The ideas are grouped and then compared with established principles and practices obtained beforehand by the tutor.

The key aspect of designing this type of material is to get the group to form concepts which enable them to understand existing objectives, procedures or principles.

For example, within the topic of farm safety, a drawing of a tractor on its side was shown. One group suggested 20 possible causes for this accident as shown in the list.

1.  Steep hill.
2.  Turned too sharply.
3.  Moving over steep slope at right angles.
4.  Speed.
5.  Towing hitch too high.
6.  Rear lift not counterbalanced.
7.  Unsafe use of fore loader i.e. too high.
8.  Knocked over by another vehicle.
9.  Projections in the ground.
10. Wrong wheel width for uneven ground.
11. Reversed into something.

## Method 4

# Using the causes of problems

12. Hit a bank.
13. Faulty machine.
14. Neglected machine, loose wheel, poor maintenance.
15. Bad, unbalanced or unlocked brakes.
16. Puncture on a slope.
17. Fell off silage clamp.
18. Too close to ditch.
19. Dirty footplate.
20. Unattended tractor out of control.

After looking at a number of different drawings of various farm accidents, the total number of concepts were used to develop a comprehensive set of safety rules, generated by the group.

The advantages of using this approach are:

The responsibility for learning lies with the learner.

The learners are participating actively in the learning process.

The learning is related to and uses the learner's experience and knowledge.

Its context is general - not restricted to "causes of problems".

This approach could be used for considering:

Safety on the road.
Safety in the home.
Safety in the office.
Safety in the factory.
Social problems.
Work practices.
Environmental issues.

# Method 5

## Using comparisons

One of the most widely used ways of increasing understanding is through comparing and contrasting. When designing training material we can carefully select things for learners to compare so that they gain broader insights.

For example, asking managers to compare and contrast an appraisal interview with a disciplinary interview gave valuable insights, as did asking young people to compare and contrast going for an interview with acting a part on the stage.

One can also learn through comparing perfect diagrams with faulty ones and having spotted the differences, to work out the consequences.

To help plumbing students understand the cold water storage system, for instance, a correct diagram was shown with all the parts labelled. Learners were asked to compare and contrast this with a number of faulty diagrams and decide what was the fault and what the effect would be. After checking their ideas they listed the principles of a cold water storage system.

Again, this method involved the learners, shared their experience and integrated the learning with what they knew already.

The answers are **never** scored or marked, but model answers are provided when the learners ask for them. They can then learn from their mistakes and consolidate their learning.

**Method 6**

# Insight through experience

The following familiar training methods are popular and effective precisely because people are actively involved in experiencing them.

Role playing

Simulations

Business games

Outward bound courses

Work experience

The key point about developing understanding through experience is that the trainer structures the experience so that the learning principles can be drawn out afterwards by course participants.

It is important for participants to complete the learning cycle through reflection and developing ideas which can be tried out.

# Developing understanding through group involvement

In the Introduction, experience was described as the culmination of past learning. This can be very useful to the individual, but can be that much greater if the sum of a number of people's experience and ideas can be tapped.

A major criticism that could be levelled at some past training is that no account was taken of the existing knowledge, skills and experience within a group and training was often a question of listening to the trainer.

Much training in the past ended without giving any transfer from the training to the job so that people were not able to transfer theory to practice.

Developing understanding through group involvement does not end with new ideas and ways of looking at things, but asks how the group can apply what has been learned. It therefore projects the learning into future activities and encourages the development of a responsible, adaptive, proactive workforce; all of these qualities have been described as necessary to deal with the kind of changes that will be increasingly met in terms of markets, products, technology, systems and organisation of work.

This section outlines how workshops can be used as consultative tools by managers in involving the workforce in the processes of change. It covers:

**Is a workshop appropriate?**
**Why involve people?**
**Designing the content of the workshop**
**Designing the processes to be used**
**A process for encouraging active learning & understanding**
**Working with the group's ideas; clustering, cause & effect, ranking**
**Action planning**

# Is a workshop appropriate?

Before you begin this section, consider some of the problems you will face if you are engaged in the processes or consequences of involving people, helping them to understand and change behaviours.

Ask yourself:

```
          Are you clear about          No
          the area of          ──────────────┐
          improvement you                     ▼
          want to tackle?            ┌──────────────────────┐
                                     │                      │
                                     │    Clarify ideas     │
              Yes                    │                      │
               ◄─────────────────────┴──────────────────────┘

          Does it just involve        Yes
          passing on facts?   ──────────────┐
                                            ▼
                                  ┌──────────────────────┐
                                  │  Use a presentation or│
              No                  │  handout with questions│
                                  └──────────────────────┘

          Is the outcome              Yes
          already decided?    ──────────────┐
                                            ▼
                                  ┌──────────────────────┐
                                  │  Restrict design of the│
                                  │  workshop to           │
              No                  │  understanding the effects│
               ◄──────────────────│  and implications      │
                                  └──────────────────────┘

          Are you prepared to         No
          give the necessary time to ──────────────┐
          design and test the workshop             ▼
          and follow up ideas, feed-      ┌──────────────────────┐
          back and action plans?          │                      │
                                          │  Do not go any further│
              Yes                         └──────────────────────┘
               ▼
       ┌──────────────────────┐
       │  Design the workshop  │
       └──────────────────────┘
```

94

# Is a workshop appropriate?

If you still want to proceed there are other factors to consider.

The process can take time because people need to look at things from different angles, accept other people's viewpoints, absorb information and relate everything to their own experience. When this has happened they then have to think about how they can contribute to making things happen, whether this relates to safety, quality, working arrangements or some other matter.

Another limitation is the number of people who can be involved at any one time. Up to 20 in a group is possible, but 10 or 12 is preferable. Where a hundred or more people are to be involved in the change then a number of workshops need to be run and again management time is an issue.

**Involving people skilfully generates energy and enthusiasm.**

**Not using their contributions produces cynicism and reluctance to co-operate in the future.**

# Why involve people?

**Concepts, unlike facts, cannot easily be told directly. We have to use various ways of helping people to form them for themselves.**

## Pitfalls

"I keep telling them we must improve our safety performance but nothing seems to happen."

"The company's objectives are clearly stated but the supervisors do not relate them to their own objectives."

"During my lecture I build up the model carefully with clear overlays, but no one uses it."

"I told them I wanted a quality job and look what they have produced."

"He's been a manager for 20 years so he must know all about managing."

## Remedies

Involve people so that they can expand their ideas and if change is needed they can contribute their knowledge and experience to shaping the necessary activities and carrying them out.

# Designing the content of the workshop

**The value of the output of a workshop depends largely on the input of the design.**

## Pitfalls

"We get a lot of participation, so we don't have to worry too much about the design."

"It will be all right on the night."

"I am at my best thinking on my feet."

"I use any old question to get them going and then I can sit back."

"There is no need to spend much time on the design, because the whole thing is so simple."

## Remedies

Remember that the purpose is to design a workshop to help people understand and implement new ideas. Take as much time, therefore, as needed to design and, wherever possible, trial the workshop.

Design with particular care the precise questions to be asked and the sequence in which to ask them.

97

# Designing the content of the workshop

## 1. Be clear about the objectives

What do I want the group to understand? (e.g. safety.)

What outcome do I want? (e.g. their involvement in behaving safely.)

How can I measure what learning has taken place? (e.g. changes in behaviour, reduced incidents.)

How much knowledge and experience does the group have? (e.g. previous lectures, training and work experience.)

## 2. Formulate some questions

The design of the questions and the order in which they are given is derived from experimental work on ways of developing understanding.

Questions based on Purpose, Comparison, Viewpoints, Problems and Checks are called "keys to understanding" and have been referred to in Principle 7 and Section 4.

**Purpose questions** clarify the group's shared understanding and give motivation to the workshop.

**Examples:**   What are the reasons for providing equal opportunities?

Why do companies advertise?

# Designing the content of the workshop

**Comparison and viewpoint questions** enlarge ideas by linking together different parts of our database. These questions are not often asked in training but should be included as they are an important means of expanding the group's concepts, in particular by:

Giving helpful insights e.g. planning a disciplinary interview is given considerable thought and care whereas planning for an appraisal interview is frequently omitted. A disciplinary interview is important, but an appraisal interview is about long-term development.

Allowing stereotypes to be examined. For example, where craftsmen were to be retrained as process workers, among the questions used were "How do process workers look to craftsmen?" and "How do craftsmen look to process workers?"

**Examples of viewpoints:**
> How is an appraisal system *viewed by* the employees?

> How does our safety programme *look to* the community?

**Examples of comparing and contrasting:**
> How will the new model be *similar to or different from* the old model?

> How does the new work organisation *need to differ* from the present one?

> How is training *similar to and different from* managing?

> In what ways is a disciplinary interview *similar to and different from* an appraisal interview?

# Designing the content of the workshop

**Problem questions** focus the group back to the subject.

It is very tempting to start a workshop with a problem question such as "Why is our reject level so high?" However, the ideas will be limited to those the group members already had when they came to the workshop. If they are encouraged to contribute their thoughts on "The purpose of measuring reject levels" and "How a reject is similar to or different from a perfect", they will be able to rethink and broaden their ideas. This leads to constructive suggestions to remedy the causes of the perceived differences between rejects and perfects. It may even reveal that their standards are out of line with company standards.

**Examples:** What could prevent us achieving BS EN ISO 9000?

What are all the things that could prevent the induction programme meeting its objectives?

What stops us from having a better safety record?

What prevents the production run taking less time?

Following the identification of problems the group can then be split up to formulate action plans.

**Checking questions** can be used to test out ideas, ask what measures need to be put into place, consider implications and check understanding.

# Designing the content of the workshop

### 3. Reviewing the design

The following list can be used to check out your workshop design:

**Ask yourself:**

1.  What is the purpose of what I am trying to do?

2.  What do I want to achieve as a result of what I am doing?

3.  Who are the questions for?  Have I assumed knowledge or experience?

4.  Am I beginning at the beginning, or rushing into conclusions or action plans too early?  (To avoid this begin a stage back from the one which seems to be the starting point.)

5.  What keys are relevant? Is there a common idea of the topic or should I begin with asking for a definition and then check understanding?

6.  Have I designed relevant questions for each key which:

    • do not include other keys

    • expand people's ideas

    • avoid the use of personal pronouns in "purpose" questions

# Designing the content of the workshop

- in viewpoint questions, specify the person or group whose viewpoint is being considered

- do not lead to, or show there is a desired answer

- avoid judgemental values

- are clear, not over complicated, or ambiguous, but at the same time prompt thoughtful answers

- do not call forth the same responses as another question but build the database from question to question

- are couched in an open-ended manner to allow people to think more broadly

- are within the capacity and experience of people to think about the answer

- are free of jargon?

7. Have I explored at least two keys, which precede "What are the problems?" before moving into action plans?

8. Have I talked the questions over with someone else? Sometimes people can read criticism or required action into the phrasing of a question, e.g. "Why should financial incentives reward safety?". Other words such as "must" and "need" should be used with discretion.

9. Have I arranged a trial run with a safe group?

10. Did I achieve my purpose in the trial run or what changes should I make?

# Designing the content of the workshop

## General points

a)  Initially it is helpful to write a number of questions around each key and later review, refine and simplify them.

b)  Introducing some questions which look outside the organisation is helpful in expanding ideas.

c)  "Why" and "What" questions are often most useful to establish purpose; "How" questions are most useful in open-ended broadening of ideas or posing problems. "Who", "When" and "Where" tend to narrow things down to identification of people, time and place.

d)  Distinguish carefully between the keys which develop understanding and actions plans which arise as a result of using the keys.

One important aspect of adult learning is that learners should feel a need to learn (Principle 1). Many people are asked to attend training events or workshops without much idea of why. Often they feel it may be some sort of punishment or signal that they have not been performing well.

To overcome this often apathetic or negative perception it is helpful to start any workshop with the question:

**"What would you like to get out of this workshop?"**

# Designing the content of the workshop

The answers can be written by people on flip chart paper and put on the wall along **with** the presenter's objectives. This shows the group, from the start, that it is a serious workshop and makes them think there may be something in it for them. If the responses are in terms of "Have no idea", "To get off the night shift" or "For a free lunch" one knows that the group is not going to be easy.

It is important **not to give any evaluative comments at all. Just listen.**

Where more relevant comments such as "To know about safety", "To understand the new structure" are made, the workshop leader makes no evaluative comments but tells the group that at the end of the workshop they will be thinking about what they have learned and will be asked to match this against their initial objectives.

Each workshop should end with two questions.

**"What have I learned from the workshop?"**
(This will make people search their minds for what they knew **before** and then compare it with the content of the session.)

**"How might I apply what I have learned?"**
(This makes people think about how they will use the ideas in the future.)

> **Too many training programmes and workshops
> seem to assume people have no previous
> experience and no need to use the ideas later.**

The relationship of objectives to end learning and the development of ideas through the pattern of key questions (purpose, viewpoints, problems, actions) enables everyone to have a sense of progress towards their goals. This is another important part of Principle 1.

# Designing the processes to be used

Besides the actual **content** of the workshop which, in addition to questions based on the **keys to understanding**, could also include presentations, problems to solve and simulations, the **processes** to be used are important. This section outlines some of the processes that can be used to meet the needs stated in six of the ten principles of learning introduced on page 32:

| | |
|---|---|
| Principle 2 | The learning environment has to be one of trust, respect, openness and acceptance of differences. |
| Principle 3 | Being aware of and owning the responsibility for learning lies with the learner. Others can only give information, support and provide feedback. |
| Principle 4 | Learners need to participate actively in the learning process. |
| Principle 5 | Learning is related to and uses the learner's experience and knowledge. |
| Principle 9 | For learning to be processed and assimilated, time must be allowed for reflection. |
| Principle 10 | Effective learning depends on realistic, objective and constructive feedback. |

# Designing the processes to be used

**It is important to channel and focus thoughts
so that ideas are offered and do not get lost**

## Pitfalls

"Let us discuss the problems on the production line."

"Come on, I want to hear everyone's ideas."

"The trouble is that once old George starts no one else can get a word in edgeways."

"Well, we haven't taken notes but I'm sure everyone has a good idea of what was suggested."

"I often have an idea but no one seems to listen."

# Designing the processes to be used

## Remedies

Questions for everyone to address must be carefully designed to meet the purpose of the workshop/meeting.

Avoid closed questions, (those which can be answered by, for example, "yes" or "no"). See pages 85 and 86.

Let pauses occur to allow people time to marshall their thoughts.

Encourage the development of ideas by letting members of the group know all their ideas will be listened to.

Encourage more ideas by letting participants know that everyone is expected to contribute. This naturally occurs through pair working. (See pages 109-110).

Collect ideas systematically going round the group.

Record all ideas verbatim.

If the meaning of an idea is unclear, encourage the individual or pair to clarify it.

Accept all ideas without praise or criticism.

Leave consideration and discussion until all ideas have been collected.

# Designing the processes to be used

**Comments which evaluate, whether negatively or positively, suppress other people's contributions when ideas are being collected from a group**

## Pitfalls

"When she told Tom that his idea showed he had completely misunderstood the question I decided not to say anything."

"Jim was congratulated on his idea but nothing was said about George's and Robert's ideas so I decided to say the same as Jim."

"They kept criticising what I said so I did not make any more suggestions."

"She tells everyone their ideas are splendid, I think she is a real con."

"The instructor praised everyone's ideas but mine, I don't usually give my ideas and I certainly won't again."

# Designing the processes to be used

## Remedies

Form the group into pairs, one effect of which is that ideas are shared and no individual feels attacked when ideas are eventually discussed. (Learning is their responsibility and they are participating actively in the learning process.)

Only query any idea if, as it is expressed, it is not understood and needs clarification.

Make **no evaluative comment** while collecting and writing up ideas. (This demonstrates respect and acceptance of differences.)

When all the ideas have been collected, encourage the group to discuss and evaluate them. Make sure there is ample time for this as it is part of the reflective learning phase.

Do not be seen to cut short the review of ideas. Remember the importance of realistic, objective and constructive feedback.

# A process for encouraging active learning and understanding

## The method involves:

1.  Explaining both the purpose of the exercise and also that a special procedure will be used to ensure that all views are heard and recorded. (Principle 4)

2.  Listening before giving information.

3.  Asking a question or questions which are neutral, do not lead and have been carefully constructed to develop understanding. (Principle 5)

4.  Pairing people to discuss each question. This generates more ideas and ensures that each individual can develop ideas and share them in a non-threatening way. The pairs use work-sheets in order to clarify their ideas in writing, but these work-sheets are not collected or the pairs identified. (Principle 4)

5.  Asking each pair in turn to state one of their ideas, until all ideas have been said. All ideas are written on flip charts, which is highly motivating to participants as it acknowledges the importance of their views. This record of all the ideas can be typed up without being modified and given back to the group as a whole. (Principles 2, 3, 4)

6.  No evaluation being made, either positively or negatively, at this time. Where, however, the ideas are not clear then further explanation or clarification should be asked for. (Principle 2)

# A process for encouraging active learning and understanding

7. Recording on the flip chart, which can be done personally by the trainer or supervisor running the session. This is important to ensure that the trainer is seen to be fully committed to the process of listening to the ideas and recording them. In other instances, such as management groups, participants can take turns at recording on the flip chart. (Principle 2)

8. When every point has been collected, which may involve going back to each pair several times, a number of things can be done. The ideas will be discussed or, if appropriate, grouped. A handout can then be provided by the trainer and the group can be asked to compare and contrast the two lists. (Principles 9 and 10). The Workshop Leader can then discuss any new points that have arisen. On other occasions, where two questions are being addressed, it might be best to collect the answers to both before distributing handouts and entering into discussion.

9. Workshop Summary

   Pair working.

   Acceptance and recording of all points **without evaluation**, but clarification can take place.

   Systematic and disciplined collection of responses from all the pairs.

   No discussion of the ideas takes place until the above requirements have been met. However **time must be allowed** for discussion afterwards.

   Input from the group leader and any handouts always follow responses from the group.

   Where action would logically follow, action plans should be developed.

# A process for encouraging active learning and understanding

Initially the people involved may be suspicious if they are not used to being asked to contribute in this way. It is therefore important to emphasise that their written notes will not be collected nor their comments identified, as the typed-up flip charts represent the views expressed by the entire group. No assessment is involved, as the process is to help share views and understanding and to clarify issues so that they can be dealt with.

**The processes are simple and powerful, but must be used with thought and care.**

## Pitfalls

**The following can lead to difficulties in workshops:**

Not giving enough thought to the formulation of questions.

Not giving enough thought to what one is going to do with the information collected.

Not allowing sufficient time.

Leading questions.

Asking too many questions.

Allowing too much time for answering questions. Keep it to about 5-10 minutes.

Not recording what people want recorded.

Not collecting ideas systematically.

Allowing discussions or evaluation of ideas as they are collected.

Cutting short collection of ideas.

Not allowing enough time for discussion of ideas after their collection.

Not acting on action plans.

# Working with the group's ideas

In some cases where the purpose of the group exercise is to develop understanding about a particular topic, e.g. what is a Quality Company, the processes of collecting ideas and discussing them are not designed to lead to any particular action or outcomes.

In this case simply getting everyone's thoughts out, discussing them and comparing them with other lists of ideas may be sufficient to help people to deepen their insight into a particular topic.

In other situations the group may be working on a particular issue or problem and the group members will expect that some actions will be taken about the issues they have raised. Because they have been involved in formulating the ideas, they will usually want to be involved in developing the actions.

A group might rightly complain if their manager listened to their ideas and collected them very systematically and then simply rolled up the flip charts and that is the last that they ever heard of their ideas. This is potentially more destructive than not involving people at all.

It can be very difficult for a group leader to handle the more open-ended part of the group discussion and manage the process so that the group identifies appropriate and realistic actions.

These are some of ways of working with the group's ideas to identify actions. Any technique you use will depend on the group, complexity of the problem and the time available. If the solution is blindingly obvious to everyone, you don't need to go through much analysis, just test out that it is the best solution. If, however, there are lots of options then they need sorting out into manageable chunks.

# Working with the group's ideas

## Clustering

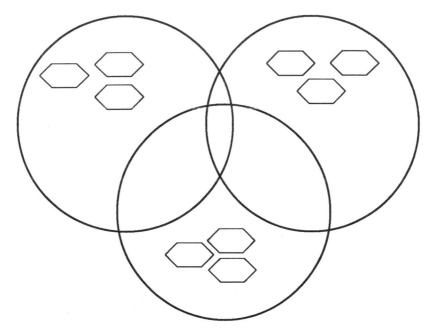

Grouping ideas and thoughts into clusters is one of the simplest ways of making a large number of ideas more manageable. This can be helped by putting each idea on a "Post It" note or postcard, then grouping them into common areas, e.g. similar problems, and giving that area a title or label. If there can be interaction between group members in the process of clustering this helps them to continue to work on ideas and see how ideas fit together. It can also be helpful to cluster ideas according to the timescale for dealing with them, e.g. things we need to work on now, soon, medium and long term.

One useful clustering method is to use magnetic hexagon shapes on which ideas can be written. This allows ideas to be fitted together and to be easily moved about as new insights emerge.

# Working with the group's ideas

## Cause and effect diagram

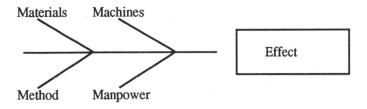

The use of a "cause and effect" or "fish bone" diagram is well recognised as a Quality Tool and is another form of clustering ideas. It provides a helpful way of sorting and grouping ideas to show how causes and effects are linked. It is a very useful approach for problem-solving and getting to the root cause.

The first stage is to decide what effect it is you would like to explore.

The questions which you design for use in the discussion can help to focus on particular problems, e.g. "What are all the reasons why this process keeps breaking down?"

Ideas are then collected on the different "bones" of the fish. In some cases it is useful to use standard labels for each of the bones as illustrated above.

# Working with the group's ideas

## Ranking

Ranking items can be a helpful way of deciding priorities for action and identifying what people feel is the best use of their time and effort at the moment.

Before ranking it may be worth discarding items over which the group will have absolutely no influence in practical terms. For example, a list of items drawn up by teachers might relate to the National Curriculum, the Government, social conditions and the economy. While these are important factors, a small group of teachers will not be able to significantly influence them so it may be better to agree to omit them at this stage.

There are two particularly useful approaches to use when ranking.

The first is to allow each group member to vote on all the ideas/ issues that have been generated. For example, if there was a list of issues that needed to be addressed, each member in the group could be invited to allocate three votes to their priority items. This can allow people to support their own issues but not allow powerful and outspoken group members to dominate the selection process. This approach ensures everyone feels that their views count equally. Usually three or four issues rise to the surface. The group's attention can then focus on looking for actions to take.

Another approach to ranking issues is to use a priority matrix:

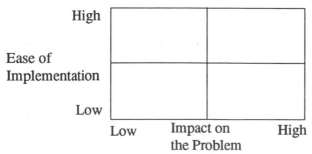

# Working with the group's ideas

## Ranking

In this matrix we consider whether a possible solution is easy to implement versus whether it will have a significant impact on the problem that we are trying to solve. If each idea is numbered the number can be positioned on the matrix drawn on a flipchart.

One useful thought when prioritising problems is to try to find the key domino issue, i.e. not all possible solutions are equally relevant. There may be one or two which if they are solved would impact on all the others.

## Action Planning

When agreeing actions in a group it is important to ensure that:

- the actions to be taken are clear and unambiguous.

- responsibilities for actions are agreed and are not shared or divided.

- there is agreement to the timescale for working on actions.

- the priority of actions (high, medium, low) is agreed.

- odds or percentage likelihood are given for the actions being carried out, which provokes realistic discussion.

- any actions to be taken by people outside the group should be communicated to and accepted by them, or an explanation given why acceptance is not possible.

- a process is put in place to review progress and update the plan.

# An example of a workshop: "working safely in times of change"

A restructuring within a large chemical organisation involved removing demarcations and introducing team working. This included more personal responsibility for aspects such as problem solving, quality, safety and environmental issues. One of the main factors holding back the changes was the fear on the part of the workforce that safety would become secondary and thereby jeopardised.

The management decided to lay the foundations for the future relationships needed to make restructuring work by involving the workforce in discussions aimed at facing problems and their solutions together.

A manager and consultant worked together to design this workshop in line with the principles and methods described in this book.

It is designed so that when the workshop begins, participants first write down their objectives for attending the workshop and these are pinned round the room together with the workshop objectives. The workshop premise is that participants have the most to offer towards any given subject that affects them. Therefore, participants, often in pairs, decide and write down on worksheets their answers to a series of core questions designed to expand and draw out views. Where remedies are needed, action plans are also drawn up by participants.

Where appropriate, handouts are distributed to give prepared responses to any of the questions asked of participants, but these always follow the gathering and discussion of views from the participants. The handout is then compared and contrasted with the views of the group. The handout is not designed to be the "correct" answer, but, where neccessary, to expand the ideas of the group and help them to see how much their ideas correspond to the views of others.

A summary of the workshop follows which outlines its content, objectives and timings, together with brief tutor's notes and some of the responses collected for each worksheet.

The intention of this section is, therefore, to give a practical example to help those who may wish to design their own workshops.

# Objectives and programme of a workshop:

**"Working safely in times of change"**

Session 1: Individual and workshop objectives (the latter being:     30 mins

- to stimulate an interest in and personal responsibility for working safely, particularly when the structure and content of jobs are altering continuously
- to develop actions that ensure we continue to work safely when changes occur).

Individual objectives are their responses to the question, "What would I like to get from this workshop?"

Session 2: The purpose of working safely     30 mins

Session 3: Things affected by change     30 mins

Session 4: Effects of change on working safely     45 mins

Session 5: Individual safety plans     30 mins

Session 6: Discussion and combination of views from     30 mins
Sessions 4 and 5, including:
i) When changes occur, how are we going to ensure these ideas are used and added to as needed?
ii) Who should be told of these ideas?

Session 7: Review     30 mins

# Tutor's notes on workshop sessions

Prepare a sufficient number of folders which contain a title page, programme and the core question themselves, each on a single sheet of paper. In some circumstances descriptive matter may be included which explains the background to any question but does not give answers.

If it is decided that handouts are beneficial, these are given out by the workshop tutor at the end of the sessions to which they refer. The content of the handouts can be obtained from a number of sources, such as text books, articles and a consensus view from management. If a number of similar workshops are being conducted, handouts can also contain or consist of the views of preceding workshops.

The following notes cover the salient points in each session after general introductions.

### Session 1

Go through workshop objectives and any housekeeping arrangements. Give each participant a half-sheet of flip chart paper and a pen. Make sure you have one yourself. Ask individuals to transfer their objectives from Worksheet A, "What would I like to get from this workshop?" onto their half-sheets and put these on the wall. The answers give an insight into what is unsettling people; the aim of the workshop is to surface all the fears and points of disquiet and give a forum for sensibly discussing them and then a mechanism for dealing with them.

### Session 2

Divide the group into pairs and ask the pairs to consider and discuss the question "What is the purpose of working safely? What is in it for me?" Ask the pairs to write their findings on Worksheet B. Allow five to ten minutes only. Collect one response in turn from each pair, without comment, until all are recorded. At this point full discussion takes place.

## Session 3

Ask the pairs to think of things affected by change, both within and outside the workplace. This is to broaden views and emphasise the fact that first, change is a perpetual phenomenon and not an isolated occurrence and that, secondly, change has some purpose. Ask the pairs to write their findings on Worksheet C, "List all the things you can think of that are being affected by change". Allow five to ten minutes only. Again, get one view from each pair until all views are recorded. Discussion can then follow, after which the handout "Change which affects the workplace" (see page 126) is distributed, or the handout can be given before the general discussion.

## Session 4

Having broadened out with the general question in Session 3, this session relates change specifically to safety. Ask the pairs to discuss the question "How might change affect my safe working?" and write their findings on Worksheet D. Again only allow five to ten minutes. Collect responses as before and record them without comment. The general discussion which follows will identify a number of the fears and worries associated with both change and safety. Then ask the pairs to consider two further questions, aimed at finding some answers to the fears and worries: "What can people do about working safely in your area when change takes place?" and "What help would people need to do these things?" Follow the same procedure as before, asking pairs to write their findings on Worksheet E (a) and E (b) respectively. Collect and then discuss responses for each worksheet.

## Session 5

To underline the mix of working group and personal responsibility, this session involves individual responses to the question "What can I do to ensure that I continue to work safely when changes occur?" Go round the group collecting individual responses on Worksheet F. Ask the group to discuss its conclusions.

## Session 6

This consists of group discussions on the material from Sessions 4 and 5. Additional material, where relevant, can be introduced by or from managers to round out the picture and help in considering two questions: a) When changes occur, how are we going to ensure these ideas are used and added to as needed? b) Who should be told of these ideas? All the views should be combined and recorded. (N.B. This session would normally culminate in action plans devised by the participants to include a description of the problems expressed, the actions to overcome these, who should take the actions, by when these should be completed, the priority of each problem and an estimate of the likelihood of actions being carried out.)

## Session 7

This session allows time for reflection on what has taken place and what actions will follow. It takes the form of participants individually completing Worksheet G, "What have I learned from the workshop?" and from the final review by participants and the tutor. Where possible their responses should be compared with their individual responses at the start of the workshop when they stated their objectives.

Following the workshop, the recorded responses and any action plans must be typed up and circulated to participants and others concerned. All the data collected should lead towards further discussions specifically aimed at handling change issues, but success can only be achieved if the process is continuous.

It is important to keep senior managers informed of progress by issuing minutes or notes of each meeting, so that the feelings and thoughts that have been brought to the surface are acted upon quickly and if not, sensible reasons given to the group why actions may be delayed or not acted upon.

# Examples of responses from worksheets

Four replies to Worksheet A, Session 1, **"What would I like to get from this workshop?"**

1. Other people's ideas on what safety is.

2. How to make my work area a safer place to work in.

3. How the changes will affect **my** safety.

4. What any new laws mean to me.

Four replies to Worksheet B, Session 2, **"What is the purpose of working safely?  What is in it for me?"**

1. To avoid injury or accident to ourselves or others.

2. You remain healthy - long term effects.

3. Increases overall efficiency - security of orders.

4. Would help reduce stress levels.

Four replies to Worksheet C, Session 3, **"List all the things you can think of that are being affected by change".**

1. Reduced manpower and multi-skilling.

2. Environmental issues good and bad - balance needed.

3. Plant utilisation - capacity demands of customer.

4. Pressure - production puts safety out of the window.

Four replies to Worksheet D, Session 4, **"How might change affect my safe working?"**

1. Maintenance standards could fall.

2. Suitability of people for jobs.

3. The way things are done, procedures and methods of work.

4. More people will require help. More caring.

# Examples of responses from worksheets

Four replies to Worksheet E(a), Session 4 **"What can people do about working safely in your area when change takes place?"**

1. Only do jobs they are validated for.

2. Ask questions.

3. Make sure they understand instructions.

4. To be more aware of the safety requirements of the job.

Four replies to Worksheet E(b), Session 4 **"What help would people need to do these things?"**

1. Praise for contribution.

2. Feedback.

3. Training packages/materials that are relevant and properly validated to meet the need!

4. Committed people to do the coaching and training.

Four replies to Worksheet F, Session 5, **"What can I do to ensure that I continue to work safely when changes occur?"**

1. Pass on experience.

2. Insist on proper training.

3. Understand responsibilities and respond to them.

4. Learn new tasks thoroughly.

Worksheet G, Session 7, **"What have I learned from the workshop?"**
(Responses not collected.)

# Session 3: Handout

**"Change which affects the workplace"**

1. Business - Competition is tougher and getting harder.

2. Economy - Downturns are happening more frequently and suddenly. The weakest and slowest at changing will fail.

3. Environment - Environmental standards and legislation are continuously tightening. Groups such as Greenpeace, Friends of the Earth and those concerned with local issues are all bringing pressure to bear and work must take place and adapt in this context.

4. Safety - Safety standards, both personal and legal, are continuously tightening.

5. Technical - World standards are getting increasingly more stringent and processes updated or redesigned. Both our processes and ways of working must therefore be kept up-to-date.

6. Customers - Their needs and expectations have become more exact. These must be identified and dominate everything we do to satisfy and preferably delight the customers.

7. Working practices - The total satisfaction of the customer's needs has meant the revision or scrapping of working practices which hinder or prevent such satisfaction and create an uncompetitive position.

8. Third World competition -The growth and strength of Third World competition emphasises the need to stay ahead of all competitors.

# Criteria to review training material

The learning material needed by industry and commerce comes from a variety of sources. Larger companies often get their material designed by their own training staff, or by external consultants. In these cases, it is specific to the company's needs.

In other cases, companies may buy in training packages which have a general application.

All learning material should be objectively evaluated to make sure it meets the needs. This is particularly important in the case of training packages, because of their generalised nature.

A common method of assessment of packages is to give the training for a trial period, after which the effect is evaluated. If the material is shown to meet the needs, then everyone is happy, but if it does not, then the trial period has been wasteful and costly. If a company has spent a great deal on a package, this failure may prove an unwelcome and contentious message, sometimes to the point where the assessment is ignored.

A potentially less expensive assessment may be to use other people's experiences and views of a package, but this requires very careful matching. Provided the people, tasks and environment are the same in both potential and past users of a package, then using the latter's experiences can be both time- and cost-saving.

Packages are often assessed by looking at the packaging, presentation, content and relevance and making an overall judgement on these factors. Two immediate problems come to mind, the first being the unconscious bias that good packaging and presentations exerts on an overall view. The second problem is that such an assessment ignores the implicit and inherent learning processes which account for a great deal of the eventual effectiveness of a learning package. It is possible, for example, to rote learn a quantity of material, but the package is less effective and, in some cases, such as safety, could lead to dangerous incidents if the first need is understanding.

All learning material, whether or not specifically written, should be reviewed for content, method and ideas to make sure it is as effective as possible. The following checklist has proved very useful in reviewing both external packages and in-company programmes, as it looks at process and product, relevance to needs and minimises the favourable effects of presentation.

# Checklist

This checklist has two purposes:

To assess training material designed by others, and structure feedback, either positive or negative in a clear and constructive manner.

To be used as a guide for designing training material.

1. The objectives are clear and material linked to end-usage.

2. The population for whom it is designed is defined.

3. The content matches the objectives.

4. The design is logical and cumulative.

5. Factual material is clear and, where necessary, written material is provided.

6. Conceptual material can be construed by the individuals themselves through the exercises.

7. Where there is a need to check facts and concepts, opportunities for feedback are always given.

8. There is good opportunity for the practice of skills, with

   constructive feedback and/or a model for comparison.

9. Learners have an opportunity to question and also discuss their learning with others.

10. There are measures of success.

# Postscript

The main theme of this book is that learners should be encouraged actively to learn and not sit there being taught.

The active learner is likely to be more involved, more responsible, more efficient and more ready to cope with change. The passive learner is more likely to evade responsibility, be less efficient and resist change. All of this could be seen as largely our fault for the way we have gone about not inspiring people to learn.

References to supporting research and other work have been deliberately omitted as this is a practical book not a formal text. If you want to delve deeper into any aspect the following titles are recommended:

**Adult Learning**
Malcolm S Knowles (1972) *Andragogy v Pedagogy*, New York Association Press. Especially Chapter 4 "What is Andragogy?" .

M Thorpe, R Edwards and A Hanson (eds) (1993) *Culture and Process of Adult Learning,* Routledge in association with The Open University.

**Study Skills**
D Rowntree (1993) *Learn How to Study*, Warner.

**Learning Styles**
P Honey and A Mumford (1992) *The Manual of Learning Styles*, Peter Honey, 10 Linden Avenue, Maidenhead, Berks SL6 6HB.

**Learning Organisations**
P M Senge (1993) *The Fifth Discipline*, Century Business.

**Training**
*The Mager Library* (6 titles), Kogan Page.

**Learning to Learn**
Editor, S Truelove (1992) *Handbook of Training and Development*, Blackwell. Chapter 4 by Sylvia Downs.